50 Premium International Steak Dishes

By: Kelly Johnson

Table of Contents

- Argentine Asado (Argentina)
- Filet Mignon (USA)
- Chateaubriand (France)
- Ribeye Steak with Chimichurri (Argentina)
- Bife de Chorizo (Argentina)
- T-bone Steak (USA)
- Côte de Boeuf (France)
- Wagyu Beef Steak (Japan)
- Picanha Steak (Brazil)
- Beef Wellington (UK)
- Grilled Tomahawk Steak (USA)
- Flank Steak with Salsa Verde (Mexico)
- Peppercorn Steak (France)
- Sirloin Steak with Béarnaise Sauce (France)
- Korean BBQ Galbi (Korea)
- Steak au Poivre (France)
- Australian Angus Beef Steak (Australia)
- Churrasco (Brazil)
- Carne Asada (Mexico)
- Sirloin with Roasted Garlic Butter (USA)
- Porterhouse Steak (USA)
- Steak Frites (France)
- Miso-marinated Ribeye (Japan)
- Ribeye with Roasted Shallots (France)
- Bistecca alla Fiorentina (Italy)
- Steak and Kidney Pie (UK)
- Grilled Hanger Steak (USA)
- Bife de Tira (Argentina)
- Salt Bae's Tomahawk (Turkey)
- Barbecued Beef Ribs (USA)
- Filet Mignon with Truffle Butter (France)
- Spicy Steak Tacos (Mexico)
- Teriyaki Steak (Japan)
- Rump Steak with Mustard Sauce (France)
- Braised Beef Short Ribs (USA)

- Grilled Beef Skewers (Middle East)
- Roast Prime Rib (USA)
- Rib-eye with Lemon and Capers (Italy)
- Asado de Tira (Argentina)
- Steak Diane (USA)
- Steak and Chimichurri Sandwich (Argentina)
- La Parrillada (Argentina)
- Venison Steak with Juniper Sauce (Sweden)
- Beef Bulgogi (Korea)
- Grilled Steak with Mango Salsa (Caribbean)
- Seared Bison Steak (Canada)
- Skirt Steak with Red Wine Reduction (France)
- Bistecca alla Pizzaiola (Italy)
- Beef Ragu with Pappardelle (Italy)
- Steak Tartare (France)

Argentine Asado (Argentina)

Ingredients:

- 2-3 pounds beef ribs or flank steak (preferably grass-fed)
- 1 tablespoon olive oil
- 4 cloves garlic, minced
- 1 tablespoon paprika
- 1 tablespoon ground cumin
- 1 tablespoon dried oregano
- Salt and pepper to taste
- 1/4 cup red wine vinegar
- 1/4 cup olive oil
- 1/4 cup chopped parsley
- 1 teaspoon red pepper flakes (optional)

Instructions:

1. Preheat your grill or parrilla (Argentine-style grill). Season the beef with olive oil, garlic, paprika, cumin, oregano, salt, and pepper.
2. Place the meat on the grill, cooking over indirect heat, and slow-cook for about 1-2 hours depending on the thickness of the cut.
3. While the meat is grilling, prepare the chimichurri sauce by mixing red wine vinegar, olive oil, parsley, and red pepper flakes (if using).
4. Once the beef is cooked to your desired doneness, serve it with the chimichurri sauce on the side.

Filet Mignon (USA)

Ingredients:

- 4 filet mignon steaks (6-8 ounces each)
- 2 tablespoons olive oil
- 2 tablespoons unsalted butter
- 2 cloves garlic, smashed
- 2 sprigs rosemary or thyme
- Salt and pepper, to taste

Instructions:

1. Preheat your oven to 400°F (200°C).
2. Season the filet mignon steaks generously with salt and pepper on both sides.
3. Heat olive oil in a heavy skillet over medium-high heat. Sear the steaks for 2-3 minutes on each side until browned.
4. Add butter, garlic, and rosemary (or thyme) to the pan. Continue to cook, basting the steaks with the melted butter for 1-2 minutes.
5. Transfer the skillet to the preheated oven and roast the steaks for 5-7 minutes for medium-rare or longer for your preferred doneness.
6. Let the steaks rest for 5 minutes before serving.

Chateaubriand (France)

Ingredients:

- 2 pounds center-cut tenderloin (Chateaubriand)
- 2 tablespoons olive oil
- 1 tablespoon Dijon mustard
- Salt and pepper, to taste
- 2 tablespoons unsalted butter
- 2 cloves garlic, minced
- 1/2 cup red wine
- 1/2 cup beef broth
- 1 tablespoon fresh parsley, chopped

Instructions:

1. Preheat the oven to 400°F (200°C). Season the tenderloin with salt, pepper, and a thin layer of Dijon mustard.
2. Heat olive oil in a large oven-safe skillet over medium-high heat. Sear the tenderloin on all sides until golden brown, about 2-3 minutes per side.
3. Add butter and garlic to the pan and roast the tenderloin in the oven for 20-25 minutes for medium-rare, or longer for your preferred doneness.
4. Remove the tenderloin from the skillet and let it rest. Meanwhile, add wine and beef broth to the skillet, scraping up any browned bits. Let the sauce simmer and reduce for 5 minutes.
5. Slice the tenderloin into thick pieces and serve with the sauce and chopped parsley.

Ribeye Steak with Chimichurri (Argentina)

Ingredients:

- 2 ribeye steaks (8-10 ounces each)
- Salt and pepper, to taste
- 1/4 cup olive oil
- 1/4 cup red wine vinegar
- 1/2 cup chopped parsley
- 2 cloves garlic, minced
- 1 teaspoon red pepper flakes (optional)
- 1 teaspoon dried oregano

Instructions:

1. Preheat your grill to medium-high heat. Season the ribeye steaks with salt and pepper.
2. Grill the steaks for about 4-5 minutes per side for medium-rare, or longer to reach your desired doneness.
3. While the steaks are grilling, prepare the chimichurri sauce by combining olive oil, red wine vinegar, parsley, garlic, red pepper flakes (if using), and oregano in a bowl.
4. Let the steaks rest for a few minutes before serving with a generous drizzle of chimichurri sauce on top.

Bife de Chorizo (Argentina)

Ingredients:

- 2 Bife de Chorizo (Argentine sirloin steaks, about 1-inch thick)
- 2 tablespoons olive oil
- Salt and pepper, to taste
- 1/2 cup chimichurri sauce (store-bought or homemade)

Instructions:

1. Preheat your grill to high heat.
2. Rub the Bife de Chorizo with olive oil and season generously with salt and pepper.
3. Grill the steaks for 6-8 minutes per side, depending on thickness and desired doneness (medium-rare is common).
4. Let the steaks rest for a few minutes before slicing.
5. Serve the Bife de Chorizo with chimichurri sauce on the side.

T-bone Steak (USA)

Ingredients:

- 2 T-bone steaks (1-inch thick)
- 2 tablespoons olive oil
- Salt and pepper, to taste
- 2 sprigs rosemary or thyme
- 2 cloves garlic, smashed
- 1 tablespoon unsalted butter

Instructions:

1. Preheat your grill to medium-high heat.
2. Rub the T-bone steaks with olive oil and season generously with salt and pepper.
3. Grill the steaks for 4-6 minutes per side for medium-rare, or longer if desired.
4. During the last minute of grilling, add the butter, garlic, and herbs to the steaks, allowing the butter to melt and infuse the meat with flavor.
5. Let the steaks rest for 5 minutes before serving.

Côte de Boeuf (France)

Ingredients:

- 2 bone-in rib steaks (Côte de Boeuf), about 2 pounds each
- 2 tablespoons olive oil
- 2 cloves garlic, minced
- 2 sprigs thyme
- Salt and pepper, to taste
- 2 tablespoons butter

Instructions:

1. Preheat your oven to 400°F (200°C).
2. Rub the Côte de Boeuf with olive oil, garlic, thyme, salt, and pepper.
3. Heat a heavy skillet over medium-high heat and sear the steaks for 3-4 minutes per side.
4. Transfer the skillet to the oven and roast the steaks for 20-25 minutes for medium-rare or longer for desired doneness.
5. Rest the steaks for 10 minutes before serving with a pat of butter on top.

Wagyu Beef Steak (Japan)

Ingredients:

- 2 Wagyu beef steaks (preferably A5 grade, 1-inch thick)
- 1 tablespoon olive oil
- Salt and pepper, to taste
- 1 tablespoon soy sauce
- 1 teaspoon mirin (optional)
- 1 teaspoon grated ginger

Instructions:

1. Let the Wagyu steaks come to room temperature before cooking. Heat a cast-iron skillet over medium-high heat.
2. Lightly oil the skillet and sear the steaks for 2-3 minutes on each side, depending on thickness. The goal is to get a nice crust while maintaining the tenderness of the meat.
3. In a small bowl, mix soy sauce, mirin, and grated ginger to make the sauce.
4. Drizzle the sauce over the cooked steaks and serve immediately. The Wagyu's rich marbling will provide a melt-in-your-mouth experience.

Picanha Steak (Brazil)

Ingredients:

- 2-3 pounds picanha (top sirloin cap) steak
- 2 tablespoons olive oil
- Salt and freshly ground black pepper
- 4 cloves garlic, minced
- 1 teaspoon smoked paprika
- 1 tablespoon fresh oregano (optional)

Instructions:

1. Preheat your grill to medium-high heat. If using a charcoal grill, prepare it for indirect cooking.
2. Season the picanha generously with salt, pepper, garlic, paprika, and oregano (if using). Rub the seasoning into the meat.
3. Place the picanha on the grill with the fat cap facing up. Cook for 10-15 minutes per side, rotating every 5 minutes to ensure even cooking. If you prefer a crispier fat cap, move the meat closer to the heat towards the end of cooking.
4. Let the meat rest for 5 minutes before slicing against the grain into thick slices. Serve with farofa (toasted manioc flour) and a side of vinaigrette.

Beef Wellington (UK)

Ingredients:

- 2 pounds beef tenderloin (center cut)
- 2 tablespoons olive oil
- Salt and pepper to taste
- 2 tablespoons Dijon mustard
- 8 oz cremini or button mushrooms, finely chopped
- 2 tablespoons unsalted butter
- 1/4 cup dry white wine
- 2 sheets puff pastry
- 2 oz prosciutto
- 1 egg (for egg wash)

Instructions:

1. Preheat the oven to 400°F (200°C).
2. Season the beef tenderloin with salt and pepper, then sear it in a hot pan with olive oil for 2-3 minutes per side until browned. Remove from heat and let it cool. Brush the beef with Dijon mustard.
3. In the same pan, melt butter and sauté the mushrooms until their moisture evaporates, about 5 minutes. Add white wine and cook until the mixture becomes dry. Let cool.
4. Lay out prosciutto on a sheet of plastic wrap, spread the mushroom mixture on top, and roll the beef into the prosciutto. Wrap the whole thing in puff pastry and brush with egg wash.
5. Bake for 25-30 minutes or until the pastry is golden brown. Let the Wellington rest for 10 minutes before slicing and serving.

Grilled Tomahawk Steak (USA)

Ingredients:

- 2 tomahawk steaks (about 2 inches thick)
- 2 tablespoons olive oil
- Salt and pepper, to taste
- 4 cloves garlic, minced
- 1 tablespoon fresh thyme, chopped
- 1 tablespoon fresh rosemary, chopped
- 2 tablespoons unsalted butter

Instructions:

1. Preheat your grill to high heat.
2. Season the tomahawk steaks generously with salt, pepper, garlic, thyme, and rosemary.
3. Grill the steaks over high heat for 4-5 minutes per side, then reduce the heat to medium and cook for an additional 8-10 minutes, depending on thickness and desired doneness.
4. In the final minutes of cooking, add a pat of butter on top of each steak to enhance flavor.
5. Let the steaks rest for 5-10 minutes before serving.

Flank Steak with Salsa Verde (Mexico)

Ingredients:

- 1.5 pounds flank steak
- Salt and pepper, to taste
- 1 tablespoon olive oil
- 1/4 cup fresh cilantro, chopped
- 2 tablespoons fresh lime juice
- 1 tablespoon red wine vinegar
- 1 tablespoon capers
- 2 cloves garlic, minced
- 1/2 teaspoon red chili flakes (optional)
- 1/4 cup extra virgin olive oil

Instructions:

1. Season the flank steak with salt and pepper. Heat olive oil in a grill pan over medium-high heat.
2. Grill the steak for about 4-5 minutes per side, depending on thickness, until medium-rare or your desired doneness.
3. Let the steak rest for 5 minutes before slicing against the grain.
4. To make the salsa verde, combine cilantro, lime juice, red wine vinegar, capers, garlic, chili flakes, and olive oil in a bowl.
5. Drizzle the salsa verde over the sliced steak and serve with tortillas or a side of rice.

Peppercorn Steak (France)

Ingredients:

- 2 sirloin steaks (8 ounces each)
- Salt and freshly cracked black pepper, to taste
- 2 tablespoons olive oil
- 1/4 cup brandy or cognac
- 1/2 cup heavy cream
- 1/4 cup beef broth
- 2 tablespoons unsalted butter
- 1 tablespoon fresh parsley, chopped

Instructions:

1. Season the steaks with salt and freshly cracked black pepper.
2. Heat olive oil in a large skillet over medium-high heat. Sear the steaks for 3-4 minutes on each side for medium-rare, or to your preferred doneness. Remove the steaks from the skillet and set aside.
3. In the same skillet, add brandy or cognac and let it reduce by half. Add heavy cream and beef broth, and simmer for 2-3 minutes.
4. Stir in butter and chopped parsley, then return the steaks to the skillet, spooning the sauce over them.
5. Serve the steaks with the creamy peppercorn sauce.

Sirloin Steak with Béarnaise Sauce (France)

Ingredients:

- 2 sirloin steaks
- Salt and pepper, to taste
- 2 tablespoons olive oil
- 1/4 cup dry white wine
- 1/4 cup white wine vinegar
- 1 small shallot, minced
- 3 egg yolks
- 1 tablespoon fresh tarragon, chopped
- 1/2 cup unsalted butter, melted

Instructions:

1. Preheat the grill or pan over medium-high heat. Season the steaks with salt and pepper, and cook for 3-4 minutes per side for medium-rare.
2. For the Béarnaise sauce, combine white wine, vinegar, shallot, and half of the tarragon in a saucepan. Simmer until reduced by half, then strain.
3. Whisk egg yolks and reduce mixture into a double boiler over simmering water. Gradually whisk in melted butter to form a creamy sauce.
4. Stir in the remaining tarragon and season with salt and pepper.
5. Pour the Béarnaise sauce over the cooked steaks and serve immediately.

Korean BBQ Galbi (Korea)

Ingredients:

- 2 pounds beef short ribs (flanken-style)
- 1/4 cup soy sauce
- 2 tablespoons brown sugar
- 2 tablespoons sesame oil
- 2 tablespoons rice wine
- 3 cloves garlic, minced
- 1 tablespoon fresh ginger, minced
- 1 tablespoon sesame seeds
- 1/4 cup green onions, chopped
- 1 tablespoon Korean chili paste (gochujang) (optional)

Instructions:

1. In a bowl, mix together soy sauce, brown sugar, sesame oil, rice wine, garlic, ginger, and gochujang (if using). Marinate the beef short ribs in the mixture for 3-4 hours or overnight.
2. Preheat the grill to medium-high heat. Grill the ribs for 2-3 minutes per side until tender and caramelized.
3. Garnish with sesame seeds and chopped green onions before serving. Serve with steamed rice and kimchi.

Steak au Poivre (France)

Ingredients:

- 2 steaks (preferably filet mignon or ribeye)
- 1 tablespoon black peppercorns, crushed
- 1 tablespoon olive oil
- 2 tablespoons unsalted butter
- 1/4 cup cognac or brandy
- 1/2 cup heavy cream
- Salt, to taste

Instructions:

1. Press the crushed black peppercorns into both sides of the steaks, seasoning with salt.
2. Heat olive oil in a pan over medium-high heat. Sear the steaks for 3-4 minutes per side until browned and cooked to your preferred doneness.
3. Remove the steaks from the pan and set aside. Add butter to the pan, followed by cognac. Carefully light the cognac with a long lighter to flambé and reduce by half.
4. Add heavy cream to the pan and simmer until the sauce thickens. Return the steaks to the pan, coating them in the creamy sauce.
5. Serve immediately with mashed potatoes or a side of vegetables.

Australian Angus Beef Steak (Australia)

Ingredients:

- 2 Australian Angus beef steaks (about 1 inch thick)
- Salt and freshly cracked black pepper, to taste
- 2 tablespoons olive oil
- 2 tablespoons unsalted butter
- 3 sprigs fresh thyme
- 2 cloves garlic, smashed

Instructions:

1. Preheat the grill or a cast-iron skillet over medium-high heat.
2. Season the beef steaks generously with salt and pepper.
3. Add olive oil to the skillet or grill. Cook the steaks for about 4-5 minutes per side, or until they reach your desired doneness.
4. Add butter, thyme, and garlic to the pan or skillet in the final minute of cooking. Spoon the melted butter over the steaks as they cook.
5. Let the steaks rest for 5 minutes before serving. Pair with roasted vegetables or a fresh salad.

Churrasco (Brazil)

Ingredients:

- 2 pounds flank steak or sirloin
- 2 tablespoons olive oil
- 2 teaspoons garlic powder
- 1 teaspoon smoked paprika
- 1 teaspoon dried oregano
- Salt and pepper, to taste
- 1 tablespoon lime juice
- Fresh parsley for garnish

Instructions:

1. Preheat the grill to medium-high heat.
2. Combine olive oil, garlic powder, paprika, oregano, salt, pepper, and lime juice in a bowl. Rub the mixture evenly onto the steak.
3. Grill the steak for about 5-6 minutes per side, depending on thickness, until medium-rare or your desired doneness.
4. Let the steak rest for 5 minutes before slicing it thinly against the grain.
5. Garnish with fresh parsley and serve with rice, beans, and grilled vegetables.

Carne Asada (Mexico)

Ingredients:

- 2 pounds flank steak or skirt steak
- 1/4 cup lime juice
- 2 tablespoons orange juice
- 1 tablespoon soy sauce
- 2 garlic cloves, minced
- 1/4 cup cilantro, chopped
- 1 teaspoon cumin
- 1/2 teaspoon chili powder
- Salt and pepper, to taste

Instructions:

1. In a large bowl, combine lime juice, orange juice, soy sauce, garlic, cilantro, cumin, chili powder, salt, and pepper to create the marinade.
2. Place the steak in the marinade and refrigerate for at least 2 hours or overnight.
3. Preheat the grill to high heat. Grill the steak for about 4-5 minutes per side for medium-rare, or to your preferred doneness.
4. Let the steak rest for a few minutes before slicing it thinly against the grain.
5. Serve with warm tortillas, salsa, and guacamole.

Sirloin with Roasted Garlic Butter (USA)

Ingredients:

- 2 sirloin steaks (about 1 inch thick)
- 1 head of garlic, halved
- 2 tablespoons olive oil
- 1/4 cup unsalted butter, softened
- 1 tablespoon fresh parsley, chopped
- Salt and pepper, to taste

Instructions:

1. Preheat your oven to 400°F (200°C).
2. Rub the garlic halves with olive oil, wrap in foil, and roast in the oven for 20-25 minutes until soft and fragrant.
3. Heat a cast-iron skillet or grill over medium-high heat. Season the steaks with salt and pepper.
4. Cook the steaks for 4-5 minutes per side, depending on thickness and desired doneness.
5. While the steaks cook, mash the roasted garlic and mix with softened butter and parsley.
6. Once the steaks are done, let them rest for 5 minutes and top with the roasted garlic butter before serving.

Porterhouse Steak (USA)

Ingredients:

- 2 porterhouse steaks (about 1.5 inches thick)
- Salt and pepper, to taste
- 2 tablespoons olive oil
- 2 tablespoons unsalted butter
- 3 sprigs rosemary
- 2 garlic cloves, smashed

Instructions:

1. Preheat your grill or cast-iron skillet to high heat.
2. Season the steaks generously with salt and pepper.
3. Add olive oil to the pan and sear the steaks for 3-4 minutes per side until browned and cooked to your preferred doneness.
4. In the last minute of cooking, add butter, garlic, and rosemary to the skillet. Spoon the melted butter over the steaks.
5. Let the steaks rest for 5-10 minutes before serving with a side of roasted potatoes or vegetables.

Steak Frites (France)

Ingredients:

- 2 ribeye or sirloin steaks
- Salt and pepper, to taste
- 2 tablespoons olive oil
- 1/4 cup unsalted butter
- 3 garlic cloves, smashed
- 2 sprigs fresh thyme
- 4 cups French fries (frites)

Instructions:

1. Heat a skillet over medium-high heat and cook the French fries until golden and crispy. Set aside and keep warm.
2. Preheat a large pan or grill over high heat. Season the steaks with salt and pepper.
3. Sear the steaks for 4-5 minutes per side, depending on desired doneness.
4. Add butter, garlic, and thyme to the pan in the last minute of cooking. Spoon the melted butter over the steaks.
5. Serve the steaks with the fries and a simple green salad on the side.

Miso-marinated Ribeye (Japan)

Ingredients:

- 2 ribeye steaks
- 2 tablespoons white miso paste
- 1 tablespoon soy sauce
- 1 tablespoon rice vinegar
- 1 tablespoon sesame oil
- 1 teaspoon honey
- 2 garlic cloves, minced
- 1 teaspoon grated ginger

Instructions:

1. In a small bowl, mix together miso paste, soy sauce, rice vinegar, sesame oil, honey, garlic, and ginger to create the marinade.
2. Coat the ribeye steaks with the marinade and refrigerate for at least 2 hours.
3. Preheat your grill or skillet over medium-high heat. Cook the steaks for 4-5 minutes per side for medium-rare.
4. Let the steaks rest for 5 minutes before slicing and serving.

Ribeye with Roasted Shallots (France)

Ingredients:

- 2 ribeye steaks
- Salt and pepper, to taste
- 2 tablespoons olive oil
- 4 shallots, halved
- 1 tablespoon unsalted butter
- 1/4 cup beef broth
- 1 teaspoon fresh thyme

Instructions:

1. Preheat your oven to 400°F (200°C).
2. Season the ribeye steaks with salt and pepper. Heat olive oil in a pan over medium-high heat.
3. Sear the steaks for 4-5 minutes per side until browned. Remove from the pan and set aside.
4. Add the shallots to the pan, cook for 3-4 minutes, then add butter and beef broth. Return the steaks to the pan, spooning the shallot mixture over them.
5. Transfer the pan to the oven and roast the steaks for 5-8 minutes, depending on doneness preference.
6. Let the steaks rest for 5 minutes before serving with the shallots and pan sauce.

Bistecca alla Fiorentina (Italy)

Ingredients:

- 2 T-bone or porterhouse steaks (about 2 inches thick)
- 2 tablespoons olive oil
- Salt and pepper, to taste
- 2 cloves garlic, smashed
- 1 sprig fresh rosemary
- 1 tablespoon unsalted butter
- Lemon wedges, for serving

Instructions:

1. Preheat your grill or a cast-iron skillet over medium-high heat.
2. Season the steaks generously with salt and pepper.
3. Sear the steaks for about 5-7 minutes per side, depending on thickness, for medium-rare.
4. Add garlic, rosemary, and butter to the pan in the final minute of cooking, basting the steaks with the melted butter.
5. Remove the steaks from the heat and let them rest for 5 minutes before slicing.
6. Serve with lemon wedges and a side of roasted vegetables or a simple salad.

Steak and Kidney Pie (UK)

Ingredients:

- 1 lb beef steak (chuck or sirloin), cubed
- 1/2 lb beef kidneys, trimmed and cubed
- 1 onion, chopped
- 1 carrot, chopped
- 2 tablespoons vegetable oil
- 2 tablespoons flour
- 2 cups beef stock
- 1/2 cup red wine
- 2 teaspoons Worcestershire sauce
- Salt and pepper, to taste
- 1 sheet puff pastry
- 1 egg (for egg wash)

Instructions:

1. In a large pot, heat the vegetable oil over medium heat. Brown the beef and kidneys in batches, then remove and set aside.
2. In the same pot, sauté onions and carrots until softened. Add flour and cook for 2 minutes to make a roux.
3. Gradually add the beef stock, red wine, and Worcestershire sauce. Stir to combine, and bring to a simmer.
4. Return the meat to the pot, season with salt and pepper, and simmer for 1-2 hours until tender.
5. Preheat the oven to 400°F (200°C). Pour the meat mixture into a pie dish.
6. Roll out the puff pastry and place it over the pie, trimming the edges. Brush with the egg wash.
7. Bake for 25-30 minutes until the pastry is golden and puffed. Let rest for 10 minutes before serving.

Grilled Hanger Steak (USA)

Ingredients:

- 1 lb hanger steak
- 2 tablespoons olive oil
- 2 cloves garlic, minced
- 1 tablespoon balsamic vinegar
- 1 tablespoon soy sauce
- Salt and pepper, to taste

Instructions:

1. Preheat your grill to medium-high heat.
2. In a small bowl, mix olive oil, garlic, balsamic vinegar, soy sauce, salt, and pepper.
3. Rub the mixture onto the hanger steak, ensuring it's well-coated.
4. Grill the steak for 4-5 minutes per side for medium-rare, or longer if preferred.
5. Let the steak rest for 5 minutes before slicing against the grain.
6. Serve with roasted potatoes or a crisp salad.

Bife de Tira (Argentina)

Ingredients:

- 2 Bife de Tira (flank steak or short ribs)
- Salt and pepper, to taste
- 2 tablespoons chimichurri sauce (store-bought or homemade)

Instructions:

1. Preheat your grill to medium-high heat.
2. Season the Bife de Tira with salt and pepper.
3. Grill for 4-6 minutes per side for medium-rare, depending on thickness.
4. Remove from the grill and let the meat rest for a few minutes.
5. Serve with a generous drizzle of chimichurri sauce and a side of grilled vegetables or potatoes.

Salt Bae's Tomahawk (Turkey)

Ingredients:

- 2 tomahawk steaks (about 2 inches thick)
- Salt, to taste (preferably sea salt)
- 2 tablespoons olive oil
- Freshly ground black pepper, to taste

Instructions:

1. Preheat your grill or cast-iron skillet to medium-high heat.
2. Rub the steaks with olive oil and season generously with salt and freshly ground black pepper.
3. Grill the steaks for 6-8 minutes per side for medium-rare, or longer if desired.
4. Rest the steaks for 5 minutes before slicing.
5. For an extra touch, finish with a sprinkle of flaky sea salt just before serving.

Barbecued Beef Ribs (USA)

Ingredients:

- 2 racks of beef ribs
- 1/4 cup brown sugar
- 2 tablespoons paprika
- 1 tablespoon garlic powder
- 1 tablespoon onion powder
- 1 tablespoon chili powder
- 1 teaspoon cumin
- Salt and pepper, to taste
- 1 cup barbecue sauce

Instructions:

1. Preheat your grill or smoker to 225°F (107°C).
2. Mix the dry spices (brown sugar, paprika, garlic powder, onion powder, chili powder, cumin, salt, and pepper) in a small bowl.
3. Rub the spice mixture generously over the beef ribs.
4. Place the ribs on the grill, bone-side down, and cook for 4-5 hours, basting occasionally with barbecue sauce.
5. Once the ribs are tender and the meat pulls away from the bone easily, remove them from the grill.
6. Slice and serve with additional barbecue sauce and sides like coleslaw and cornbread.

Filet Mignon with Truffle Butter (France)

Ingredients:

- 2 filet mignon steaks (about 6 oz each)
- Salt and freshly cracked black pepper
- 2 tablespoons olive oil
- 2 tablespoons unsalted butter
- 1 tablespoon truffle oil
- 1/4 cup chopped fresh parsley

Instructions:

1. Preheat your oven to 400°F (200°C).
2. Season the filet mignon with salt and pepper on both sides.
3. Heat olive oil in a skillet over medium-high heat. Sear the steaks for 2-3 minutes on each side until browned.
4. Transfer the skillet to the oven and roast the steaks for 5-7 minutes, depending on thickness and desired doneness.
5. In the final minute of cooking, add butter and truffle oil to the pan, basting the steaks with the melted butter.
6. Let the steaks rest for 5 minutes before serving, garnished with fresh parsley.

Spicy Steak Tacos (Mexico)

Ingredients:

- 1 lb flank steak or skirt steak
- 2 tablespoons olive oil
- 1 tablespoon chili powder
- 1 teaspoon cumin
- 1 teaspoon smoked paprika
- 1/2 teaspoon cayenne pepper (adjust to taste)
- Salt and pepper, to taste
- 8 small flour tortillas
- 1 cup shredded lettuce
- 1/2 cup diced tomatoes
- 1/4 cup crumbled queso fresco
- Lime wedges, for serving

Instructions:

1. Preheat your grill or skillet to medium-high heat.
2. Rub the steak with olive oil and season with chili powder, cumin, paprika, cayenne, salt, and pepper.
3. Grill the steak for 4-5 minutes per side, until medium-rare or desired doneness.
4. Let the steak rest before slicing thinly against the grain.
5. Warm the tortillas on the grill or in a pan.
6. Assemble the tacos by placing the steak slices in the tortillas, then topping with shredded lettuce, diced tomatoes, crumbled queso fresco, and a squeeze of lime juice.

Teriyaki Steak (Japan)

Ingredients:

- 2 rib-eye or sirloin steaks
- 1/4 cup soy sauce
- 2 tablespoons sake
- 2 tablespoons mirin
- 1 tablespoon brown sugar
- 1 teaspoon grated ginger
- 2 cloves garlic, minced
- 1 tablespoon sesame oil
- Sesame seeds, for garnish
- Sliced green onions, for garnish

Instructions:

1. In a small bowl, whisk together soy sauce, sake, mirin, brown sugar, ginger, and garlic to make the teriyaki marinade.
2. Place the steaks in a shallow dish and pour the marinade over them. Cover and refrigerate for at least 30 minutes (up to 2 hours).
3. Preheat your grill or skillet to medium-high heat.
4. Cook the steaks for 4-6 minutes per side for medium-rare, basting with the marinade as they cook.
5. Remove from the heat and let the steaks rest for 5 minutes.
6. Garnish with sesame seeds and sliced green onions before serving. Pair with steamed rice or sautéed vegetables.

Rump Steak with Mustard Sauce (France)

Ingredients:

- 2 rump steaks
- Salt and pepper, to taste
- 2 tablespoons olive oil
- 1/4 cup Dijon mustard
- 1 tablespoon white wine vinegar
- 1/4 cup heavy cream
- 1 teaspoon fresh thyme, chopped
- 1 tablespoon butter

Instructions:

1. Season the rump steaks with salt and pepper.
2. Heat olive oil in a skillet over medium-high heat. Cook the steaks for 4-5 minutes per side for medium-rare, or longer if desired.
3. Remove the steaks from the skillet and set aside to rest.
4. In the same skillet, add the Dijon mustard, white wine vinegar, and heavy cream. Stir and cook for 2-3 minutes until the sauce thickens.
5. Stir in fresh thyme and butter, cooking for another minute until the butter melts.
6. Serve the steaks with the mustard sauce poured over them, accompanied by mashed potatoes or roasted vegetables.

Braised Beef Short Ribs (USA)

Ingredients:

- 4 beef short ribs
- Salt and pepper, to taste
- 2 tablespoons olive oil
- 1 onion, chopped
- 2 carrots, chopped
- 2 celery stalks, chopped
- 4 cloves garlic, minced
- 1 cup red wine
- 2 cups beef broth
- 1 sprig rosemary
- 2 sprigs thyme
- 1 tablespoon tomato paste

Instructions:

1. Preheat your oven to 325°F (163°C).
2. Season the short ribs with salt and pepper. Heat olive oil in a Dutch oven over medium-high heat.
3. Brown the short ribs in batches, then remove and set aside.
4. Add the onion, carrots, celery, and garlic to the pot, cooking until softened, about 5 minutes.
5. Stir in tomato paste, then pour in the red wine to deglaze the pan. Cook for 2-3 minutes, allowing the wine to reduce slightly.
6. Return the short ribs to the pot, add beef broth, rosemary, and thyme. Bring to a simmer.
7. Cover and transfer the pot to the oven. Braise for 2-3 hours until the meat is tender and falling off the bone.
8. Serve with mashed potatoes or polenta.

Grilled Beef Skewers (Middle East)

Ingredients:

- 1 lb beef (sirloin or flank steak), cut into cubes
- 2 tablespoons olive oil
- 2 tablespoons lemon juice
- 2 teaspoons ground cumin
- 2 teaspoons ground coriander
- 1 teaspoon ground paprika
- Salt and pepper, to taste
- 1 red onion, cut into chunks
- 1 bell pepper, cut into chunks
- Skewers (soaked if wooden)

Instructions:

1. In a bowl, combine olive oil, lemon juice, cumin, coriander, paprika, salt, and pepper.
2. Add the beef cubes to the marinade, mixing to coat. Let marinate for 30 minutes.
3. Preheat your grill to medium-high heat.
4. Thread the beef, onion, and bell pepper onto the skewers, alternating between the beef and vegetables.
5. Grill the skewers for 4-5 minutes per side, or until the beef reaches your desired doneness.
6. Serve the skewers with rice or flatbread and a side of yogurt or tzatziki.

Roast Prime Rib (USA)

Ingredients:

- 1 bone-in prime rib roast (about 4-6 pounds)
- 2 tablespoons olive oil
- 1 tablespoon garlic powder
- 1 tablespoon onion powder
- 2 teaspoons fresh rosemary, chopped
- 2 teaspoons fresh thyme, chopped
- Salt and pepper, to taste
- 1 cup beef broth

Instructions:

1. Preheat your oven to 450°F (230°C).
2. Rub the prime rib roast with olive oil, garlic powder, onion powder, rosemary, thyme, salt, and pepper.
3. Place the roast in a roasting pan, bone-side down, and roast for 15 minutes at 450°F.
4. Reduce the oven temperature to 325°F (165°C) and continue roasting for 1.5-2 hours, or until the internal temperature reaches 130°F for medium-rare.
5. Remove the roast from the oven and let it rest for 15 minutes before slicing.
6. Serve with roasted potatoes and a rich gravy made from the pan drippings and beef broth.

Rib-eye with Lemon and Capers (Italy)

Ingredients:

- 2 rib-eye steaks
- Salt and pepper, to taste
- 2 tablespoons olive oil
- 1/4 cup fresh lemon juice
- 2 tablespoons capers, drained
- 1 tablespoon butter
- 1/4 cup fresh parsley, chopped

Instructions:

1. Season the rib-eye steaks with salt and pepper.
2. Heat olive oil in a skillet over medium-high heat. Sear the steaks for 4-5 minutes per side for medium-rare, or longer if desired.
3. Remove the steaks from the skillet and set aside to rest.
4. In the same skillet, add lemon juice, capers, and butter, stirring to create a sauce.
5. Cook for 2-3 minutes until the sauce is slightly thickened.
6. Serve the steaks with the lemon-caper sauce and garnish with fresh parsley.

Asado de Tira (Argentina)

Ingredients:

- 2 racks of beef short ribs (asado de tira)
- Salt and pepper, to taste
- 1/4 cup chimichurri sauce (store-bought or homemade)

Instructions:

1. Preheat your grill to medium-high heat.
2. Season the beef short ribs with salt and pepper.
3. Grill the ribs for 6-8 minutes per side, turning occasionally, until tender and slightly charred.
4. Brush the ribs with chimichurri sauce while grilling.
5. Serve the ribs with a side of grilled vegetables or potatoes and more chimichurri sauce on the side.

Steak Diane (USA)

Ingredients:

- 2 filet mignon steaks
- Salt and pepper, to taste
- 2 tablespoons olive oil
- 1 tablespoon butter
- 1/4 cup brandy
- 1/4 cup heavy cream
- 2 tablespoons Dijon mustard
- 1/4 cup fresh parsley, chopped

Instructions:

1. Season the steaks with salt and pepper.
2. Heat olive oil in a skillet over medium-high heat. Cook the steaks for 3-4 minutes per side for medium-rare, or longer if preferred.
3. Remove the steaks from the skillet and set aside.
4. In the same skillet, melt butter over medium heat. Add brandy and cook for 1-2 minutes to reduce.
5. Stir in heavy cream and Dijon mustard, cooking for an additional 3-4 minutes.
6. Return the steaks to the skillet, spooning the sauce over them, and cook for another minute.
7. Serve the steaks with the sauce and garnish with fresh parsley.

Steak and Chimichurri Sandwich (Argentina)

Ingredients:

- 1 lb flank or skirt steak
- Salt and pepper, to taste
- 1 tablespoon olive oil
- 4 crusty sandwich rolls
- 1/2 cup chimichurri sauce (store-bought or homemade)
- Sliced onions and tomatoes (optional)

Instructions:

1. Season the steak with salt and pepper. Heat olive oil in a skillet or grill pan over medium-high heat.
2. Cook the steak for 4-5 minutes per side for medium-rare, or adjust to your desired doneness.
3. Let the steak rest for 5 minutes before slicing it thinly against the grain.
4. Toast the sandwich rolls lightly. Spread chimichurri sauce on the rolls and layer with the sliced steak.
5. Add sliced onions and tomatoes if desired, and serve.

La Parrillada (Argentina)

Ingredients:

- 1 lb beef ribs
- 1 lb sausages (chorizo, morcilla)
- 1 lb flank steak
- 1 tablespoon olive oil
- Salt and pepper, to taste
- Chimichurri sauce (for serving)

Instructions:

1. Preheat your grill to medium-high heat. Season all meats with olive oil, salt, and pepper.
2. Grill the beef ribs, sausages, and flank steak for about 10-15 minutes, turning occasionally, until cooked to your preference.
3. Serve the grilled meats with chimichurri sauce on the side and enjoy with grilled vegetables or a salad.

Venison Steak with Juniper Sauce (Sweden)

Ingredients:

- 2 venison steaks
- Salt and pepper, to taste
- 1 tablespoon butter
- 1/4 cup red wine
- 1 tablespoon juniper berries, crushed
- 1/2 cup beef broth
- 1 tablespoon heavy cream

Instructions:

1. Season the venison steaks with salt and pepper.
2. Heat butter in a skillet over medium-high heat. Sear the venison steaks for 3-4 minutes per side for medium-rare.
3. Remove the steaks and set aside to rest.
4. In the same skillet, add red wine, crushed juniper berries, and beef broth. Cook for 5-7 minutes until the sauce thickens.
5. Stir in the heavy cream and cook for another minute.
6. Pour the juniper sauce over the venison steaks and serve with mashed potatoes or root vegetables.

Beef Bulgogi (Korea)

Ingredients:

- 1 lb rib-eye or sirloin steak, thinly sliced
- 1/4 cup soy sauce
- 2 tablespoons brown sugar
- 1 tablespoon sesame oil
- 2 cloves garlic, minced
- 1 tablespoon grated ginger
- 2 tablespoons rice vinegar
- 2 tablespoons gochujang (Korean chili paste)
- 2 tablespoons sesame seeds
- Sliced green onions, for garnish

Instructions:

1. In a bowl, combine soy sauce, brown sugar, sesame oil, garlic, ginger, rice vinegar, and gochujang to make the marinade.
2. Add the sliced beef to the marinade and let it sit for at least 30 minutes.
3. Heat a grill or skillet over medium-high heat. Grill or stir-fry the marinated beef for 2-3 minutes until cooked through.
4. Garnish with sesame seeds and green onions before serving with steamed rice or kimchi.

Grilled Steak with Mango Salsa (Caribbean)

Ingredients:

- 2 sirloin steaks
- Salt and pepper, to taste
- 1 tablespoon olive oil
- 1 mango, peeled and diced
- 1/4 red onion, finely chopped
- 1/2 red bell pepper, diced
- 1 tablespoon lime juice
- 2 tablespoons cilantro, chopped

Instructions:

1. Season the steaks with salt and pepper. Heat olive oil in a skillet or grill pan over medium-high heat.
2. Grill the steaks for 4-5 minutes per side, or until desired doneness is achieved.
3. While the steaks cook, prepare the mango salsa by combining mango, red onion, red bell pepper, lime juice, and cilantro in a bowl.
4. Serve the grilled steaks topped with mango salsa and a side of rice or vegetables.

Seared Bison Steak (Canada)

Ingredients:

- 2 bison steaks (such as rib-eye or tenderloin)
- Salt and pepper, to taste
- 1 tablespoon butter
- 1 tablespoon olive oil
- 2 cloves garlic, minced
- 1 sprig thyme

Instructions:

1. Season the bison steaks with salt and pepper.
2. Heat butter and olive oil in a skillet over medium-high heat. Add garlic and thyme.
3. Sear the bison steaks for 4-5 minutes per side for medium-rare, or cook to your desired level of doneness.
4. Let the steaks rest for 5 minutes before serving with roasted potatoes or a green salad.

Skirt Steak with Red Wine Reduction (France)

Ingredients:

- 2 skirt steaks
- Salt and pepper, to taste
- 2 tablespoons olive oil
- 1/2 cup red wine
- 1 tablespoon balsamic vinegar
- 1 tablespoon butter
- 1 tablespoon fresh thyme, chopped

Instructions:

1. Season the skirt steaks with salt and pepper.
2. Heat olive oil in a skillet over medium-high heat. Sear the steaks for 2-3 minutes per side for medium-rare, or longer if desired.
3. Remove the steaks and set aside. Add red wine and balsamic vinegar to the skillet, scraping up any browned bits.
4. Cook for 5 minutes until the sauce has reduced by half. Stir in butter and fresh thyme.
5. Serve the skirt steak topped with the red wine reduction sauce.

Bistecca alla Pizzaiola (Italy)

Ingredients:

- 2 beef steaks (such as rib-eye or sirloin)
- 1/4 cup olive oil
- 2 cloves garlic, minced
- 1 can crushed tomatoes (14 oz)
- 1 tablespoon dried oregano
- Salt and pepper, to taste
- Fresh basil leaves, for garnish

Instructions:

1. Heat olive oil in a skillet over medium-high heat. Add the steaks and cook for 3-4 minutes per side.
2. Remove the steaks and set aside. Add garlic to the skillet and cook for 1 minute.
3. Stir in the crushed tomatoes, oregano, salt, and pepper. Simmer for 10 minutes.
4. Return the steaks to the skillet and cook for another 3-4 minutes, allowing the steaks to soak in the sauce.
5. Serve with fresh basil and a side of pasta or bread.

Beef Ragu with Pappardelle (Italy)

Ingredients:

- 1 lb beef chuck roast, cut into chunks
- 2 tablespoons olive oil
- 1 onion, chopped
- 2 carrots, chopped
- 2 cloves garlic, minced
- 1/2 cup red wine
- 2 cups beef broth
- 1 can crushed tomatoes (14 oz)
- 1 teaspoon dried rosemary
- 1 pound pappardelle pasta
- Fresh Parmesan cheese, for garnish

Instructions:

1. Heat olive oil in a Dutch oven over medium-high heat. Brown the beef chunks in batches and set aside.
2. Add onion, carrots, and garlic to the pot, cooking until softened.
3. Deglaze the pot with red wine, then add beef broth, tomatoes, rosemary, and the browned beef.
4. Simmer for 2-3 hours, until the beef is tender and shreds easily.
5. Cook the pappardelle pasta according to package directions. Toss the pasta with the beef ragu and garnish with fresh Parmesan cheese.

Steak Tartare (France)

Ingredients:

- 8 oz high-quality beef tenderloin, finely chopped
- 1 egg yolk
- 2 tablespoons Dijon mustard
- 1 tablespoon Worcestershire sauce
- 2 tablespoons capers, chopped
- 2 tablespoons fresh parsley, chopped
- Salt and pepper, to taste
- Toasted bread or crackers, for serving

Instructions:

1. In a bowl, combine the finely chopped beef, egg yolk, Dijon mustard, Worcestershire sauce, capers, and parsley.
2. Mix well and season with salt and pepper.
3. Serve immediately with toasted bread or crackers for dipping.

www.ingramcontent.com/pod-product-compliance
Lightning Source LLC
LaVergne TN
LVHW081500060526
838201LV00056BA/2855